D0961962

I have
a surprise

SOMEDAY
A BIRD
WILL POOP
ON YOU

LIFE TROOTH SIGNS, LLC

Written by Sue Salvi
Illustrated by Megan Kellie

VORACIOUS

Little, Brown and Company

New York   Boston   London

FOR AUGIE & OSCAR
GO FORTH AND BE POOPED ON

AND FOR JOHN BLEEDEN
IMPERVIOUS TO POOPS

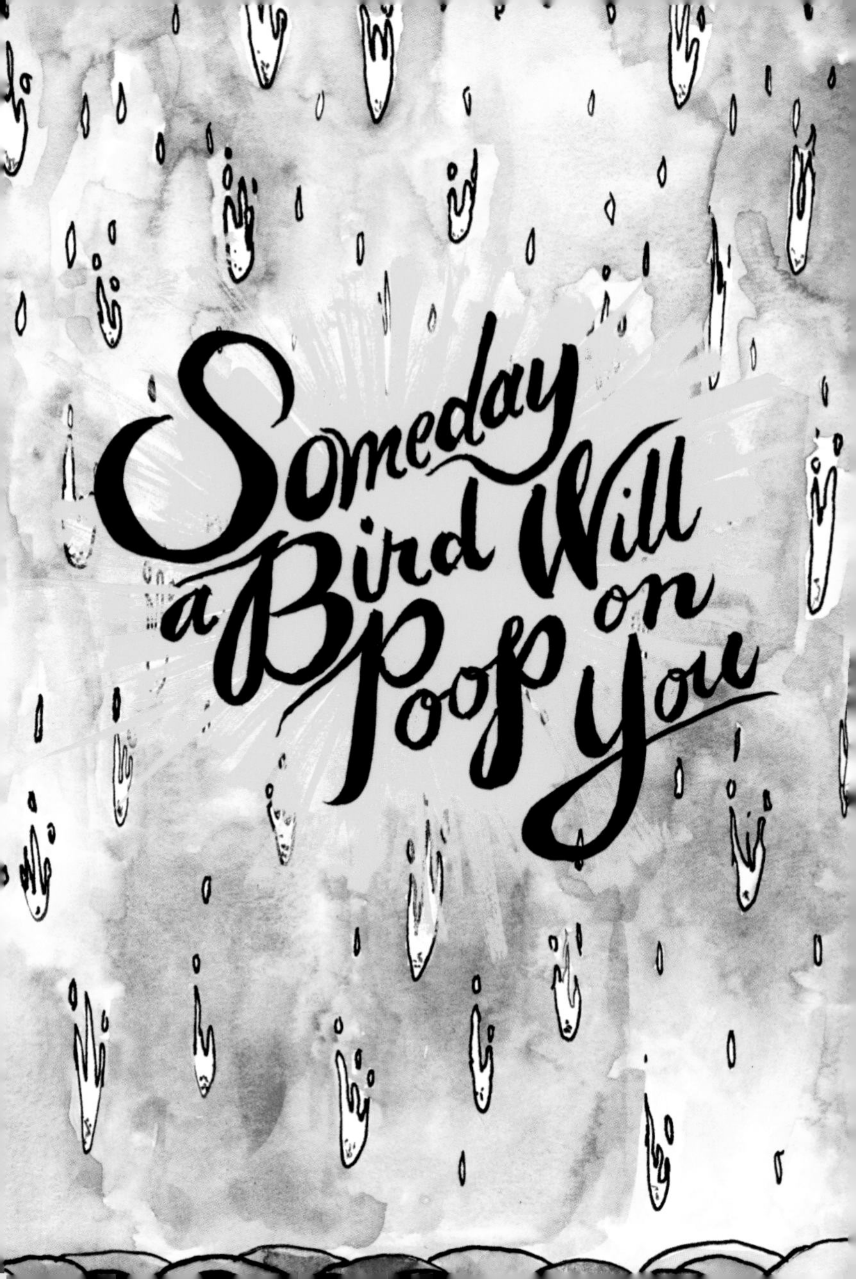
Someday a Bird Will Poop on You

Sometime, in the long life
you have ahead of you,
there will be a day
when a bird will poop on you.

YOUR LIFE

Because there are birds
up in the sky,

and there are people
down below,

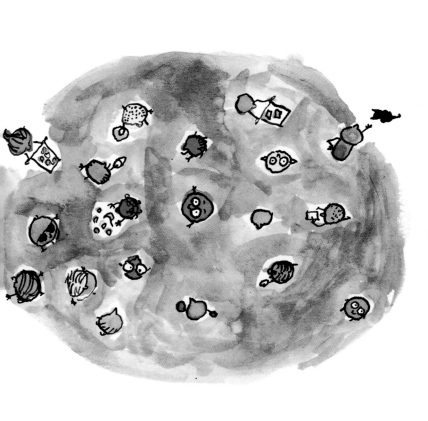

and you

are one of those people.

So it just makes sense
that someday,

you might feel something
plop on your head,

or splatter on your shoulder,

or dribble down your lapel,
if it's a lapel-wearing kind of day,

and you'll reach for it and
feel the goo that is bird poo.

That's how it happens.

It won't be on a day that you leave your house thinking, "Today I'm sure a bird will poop on me so I'll bring a change of clothes and leave early and I'll bring some bird toilet paper."

Probably every single day,
somewhere in the world,

someone is getting pooped on by a bird.

Maybe right now even,
as this book is happening
to you,

someone in China is
getting pooped on by a
Chinese bird.

Or someone in Gibraltar is getting pooped on by a Gibraltarian bird.

Or someone in Maine
is getting pooped on
by a visiting Canadian bird.

It just happens.

You won't know when.

Other than that it will be at the worst possible time.

Like the day of an important job interview.

Or the day you are flaunting
an intricate hairdo.

Or the day you're running late
to a ceremony in which
you are to receive an award

for never being late

to anything.

So...

On that day
the bird poops on you,

you have a choice:

You can get really mad.

And cry.

And stomp.

And yell, "I don't want this to happen! Raah, grahh, kerrrrr!"

And let it ruin the rest of your day.

* HOW YOU FEEL INSIDE

Or you can remain calm.
Wash it off.

Maybe laugh about it, too.

Like this: "Har har."

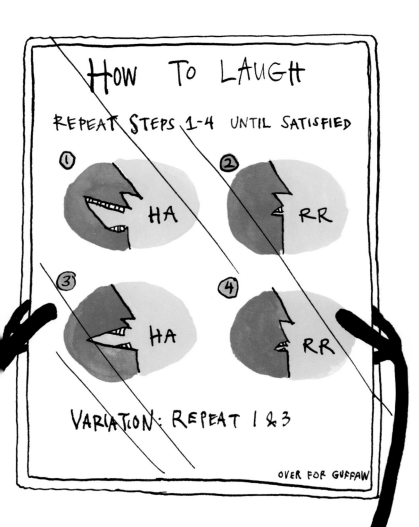

Then think to yourself:
"Now, chances are, I won't have another bird poop on me for a while."

And if one does?

What a hilarious story that will be!

The End.

Voracious / Little, Brown and Company
Hachette Book Group
1290 Avenue of the Americas, New York, NY 10104
littlebrown.com

First Little, Brown edition: October 2018
Originally published by Archer & Wolf Publishing: October 2014

Voracious is an imprint of Little, Brown and Company, a division of Hachette Book Group, Inc.
The Voracious name and logo are trademarks of Hachette Book Group, Inc.

The publisher is not responsible for websites (or their content) that are not owned by the publisher.

The Hachette Speakers Bureau provides a wide range of authors for speaking events. To find out more, go to hachettespeakersbureau.com or call (866) 376-6591.

ISBN 978-0-316-48776-4
LCCN 2018952120

10 9 8 7 6 5 4 3 2

PHX

Printed in the United States of America

Sue Salvi, *Author*

Sue cherishes the bird poops she has received including a monstrous fecal incident that happened on her left forearm, moments before speaking at an extra-sacred church event. Originally from Pittsburgh, Sue now lives in Chicago with her husband and two boys. She occasionally performs improv and sketch comedy around town. There has been a peregrine falcon in her backyard, twice so far. You may find her verbal poops on Twitter @suesalvi.

Megan Kellie, *Illustrator*

Megan is proud of the bird poops she has collected while on earth. Once, sitting in a park, she thought, "Wow, it's like I'm in a brochure," until a bird pooped on her, to let her know she was not. She lives in Chicago, is also a writer-performer person, would like to make approximately everything, and prefers low-ceilinged restaurants. She emits words on Twitter @flipflipflap and drawings on Instagram @imdrawinghere.

Special thanks to Paul Grondy, R.T. Durston, Heather Skomba, John Bleeden, Julie Regimand, Daniel Lazar, Michael Szczerban, and Ron Lazzeretti.

ACCOUTREMENTS

WHEN FILLED:
GET NEW CARD

HOW TO LAUGH

REPEAT STEPS 1-4 UNTIL SATISFIED

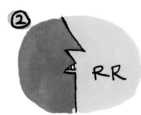

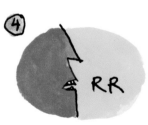

VARIATION: REPEAT 1 & 3

OVER FOR GUFFAW

HOW TO GUFFAW

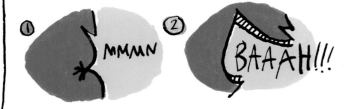